HANDS IN CLAY

HANDS IN CLAY

POEMS

MILDRED KICONCO BARYA

SERVING HOUSE BOOKS

Hands in Clay
Copyright © 2025 Mildred Kiconco Barya
First Edition

All rights reserved. No part of this book may be reproduced or transmitted in any form or by any means, electronic, digital, or mechanical, including photocopy, audio recording, or any information storage and retrieval system, without prior permission from the publisher or author (except by reviewers who may quote brief passages). No part of this book may be used or reproduced in any manner for the purpose of training artificial intelligence technologies or systems.

Cover design by Jacob Arms

Published by Serving House Books
Lawrence Landing Company
Raleigh, North Carolina 27609
United States of America

www.servinghousebooks.com

Serving House Books is a proud member of

Independent Book Publishers Association
 and
Community of Literary Magazines and Presses

Paperback ISBN: 9781947175990

Library of Congress Control Number: 2025946173

SERVING HOUSE BOOKS

CONTENTS

LIFE

My House	1
A Kingdom of Children	2
Cycles	3
The Things You Encounter in Flight	5
Roosters, Taxi, and Murakami	7
Lucky	9
Old Bartimaeus, I Feel You	10
One Plus One Equals Three	11
Devotion	12
The Goat, the City, the Embassy	14
They Birthed Nations, Word Says	15
A Very Short Story	20
The Shape of Light	21
Tasseography	22
The Baby in the Priest's Room	23
Seven of Dragons	24
In the Animal Kingdom, Mothers Feed...	25
Overload	26
Abundance	27
October	28

DEATH

The Diminishing Years	31
Integration	32
Things Have Been Disappearing	33
My Father Is a Rainbow	34
The Nature of Opposition	36
I've Kept You Alive	37
Transit 11 11	39
Leonard Cohen Saves the Maiden	40
Dad Is Happy Drinking Beer in Heaven...	41

The Movement of Bodies	42
Chthonic	43
The Sink	45
Austerity	46
A Place of Burning	47
Winters	49
Does It Get Better?	50
Blazing Wild	51
Father	52
Komorebi	53
Hands in Clay	54

REBIRTH

There's No Present but the Past...	57
House of Moab	58
Loved	59
The Tower Falls	60
You Are Here—on a Map	62
Climbing a Giant Waffle-like Building...	63
The Tools We Carry	65
The Fire People	66
Letting Go	67
Between Wake and Sleep...	69
The Boy Who Loved	71
Piano Lessons	72
To Bury a Fire	73
Growing Up	75
The Wisdom of Sea Cucumbers	76
The Future	77
Beans	79
Sanctum	80
These Moments	82
18 Notes to Finish	84
Acknowledgments	85

For my sisters, Mabel and Nancy

LIFE

My House

To weave risk and beauty in a fragile balance,
my house firm and delicate as a spider's home.

I wish for myself a house made of webs,
each thread mirroring a path I have taken

and others I'm yet to take. Each spin leading
to a room with many windows to see monarch

butterflies, and guest wings for my family
and friends. I pray that my house will be open

and airy, indestructible in its elegance and lightness.
I do not wish for permanence, but what's durably

suspended in eternal presence the way pollen grasps
bodies of strangers on their walks. The spider at work

hangs precariously over a cliff, water trickling
beneath, as though unaware of the danger.

Perhaps even inspired by it. Invisible to travelers
jumping rocks on their way to the meadows.

A Kingdom of Children

I'm often surrounded by children.

Tonight, one of them said I'm an Aquarius
even though my zodiac is Leo.

I had to be a *particular* child, said the kid,
here for a purpose. But what purpose?

Later I wondered if I'd misheard. Could
the kid have said *curious*?

Anyway, I like looking after these children
and sometimes they take care of me.

We understand each other—we've met
elsewhere before. Last night
we congregated outside the gate
of my childhood home.

We often rendezvous in indistinguishable
places—hazy mountains, foggy meadows—
walking, talking randomly, and stopping
frequently to smell the dahlias or touch
plants. Only then do I notice being older
because I start telling them to keep moving,
as if I have a specific destination in mind.

We never arrive. Maybe we're not going
anywhere. We're just a kingdom of children
ceaselessly existing beforelife or afterlife,
rapt in an expanse of playful aimlessness.

Cycles

Back home when a girl got her period,
folks would say she's seen the moon.
The way it was whispered among the elders made me
think it was a marvelous thing. Numinous. It gave me
a grand vision of womanhood, and I couldn't wait
to meet my older self that would spot the becoming
moon and say, Welcome!
Divinity is your essence.
Draw back the curtains of my bedroom,
unlatch the window and Exit, Girl Child.
Open the door with a grin, let the woman swagger.
I waited for the moon with anxious joy.
I should have been warned to be careful.
When my cycle came, I hated it.

        Among the beetles, lizards, and snakes,
        blood is expelled from the mouth, nostrils,
    and eyes, mostly for defense—*autohaemorrhage*.
Imagine surprising a lizard or snake in the woods and,
sensing a threat, eyes swell and flash faster than you
can recall there will be blood!

In my village, old men say if you drink the blood of a
horned toad, you become horny

I wish to tell them it takes just a kiss. A touch.
  A wave of desire and sometimes waking up at 3 a.m...
        taking matters into one's own hands.

Ever wonder why in the Western tradition menses
evoke the curse— demeaning and acknowledging
simultaneously a power men seek to undermine
with negative conjurations.

It is said of virgin-obsessed cultures that girls
who are no longer virgins will pack a vial of lizard
or lamb blood to sprinkle between their thighs
and sheets on their wedding night.
They'll scream and bite during lovemaking,
writhe and thrash.
And yes, they'll squirt blood.
The new husbands will comfort them
in their strong, bear-like arms
and brag about being "the first" to their friends.

It's a win-win in the cloudy ring of predator-prey
camouflage, doubling tricksters cloaked in mystery
whose Patron Saint and Queen of subversion—Biblical
Rachel—stole her father's gods and hid them in her
saddlebag, then threatened with blood and refused
to dismount: *Let not my lord be angry that I cannot
rise before you, for the way of women is upon me.*
The spell cast, the moon smiling,
Laban's idols turned to adopt a new lord and home.

The Things You Encounter on a Flight

Seated by the window, my eyes
focus on the sun emerging
through the brightening sky.
As we enter the yellow and purple
strands, my heart flutters.

I look at my neighbor to distract
her from the book she's reading,
so that she takes in this glorious
salutation. So that we talk. But how
to do so without being intrusive?
I don't want to be *that* person,
but given this occasional moment,
I'm willing to risk. We have three
hours. Surely, we can share a minute.
Statistics for the Terrified is the title
she's engrossed in. It reminds me
of how I felt about Math in high
school. I'm not scared of flying
though. In fact, I become elated
when airborne. My body relaxes,
my cells tingle, and my mind opens
to absorb the whole Universe. I
become courageous, expansive,
eager to start a conversation.
So, Hello!

Silence.

Hello! A little louder. At the same

time, I lift my elbow as if to nudge
her. She notices and smiles.
I point to the sunrise.

Huh! Loud breath escapes from her.
A hand goes to her chest. Lips stay
parted and she looks like she's
having a heart attack.

I'm a little frightened I've caused
serious harm. My morbid mind
takes over and I imagine cases
of people dying at the sight of beauty,
their hearts unable to bear it.
Fast forward, I'm talking
with a reporter who wants to know
as her seatmate if I remember what
her last seconds in air were like. I
hear her laughing, and I snap out of it.
She can't believe the sight! She's
enthralled there's a small pond
shimmering in her eyes. Her face
reminds me of a little girl's filled
with wonder. Animated by the magnificent
sunrise which has intensified—
fire in the sky, vibrant red
with orange flames amidst wisps
of royal purple. Our plane progresses
through the flames and her hand finds
mine. There's no resistance. We
hold hands without saying a word,
without turning our faces away
from the small window.

Roosters, Taxi, and Murakami

Going downtown in a public taxi, we stop briefly in Kabalagala, a popular hangout for nightlife. Passengers get on and off. An elderly woman dressed in a flowery brown and yellow gomesi enters carrying two large roosters in her arms. She sits next to me, and I suppress the urge to take a picture. Normally, I wouldn't be finding the scene comical had I not momentarily transposed it onto an RTD bus from Colorado Blvd, where I reside, to Denver University or downtown: the bus stops at Evans Avenue, and a woman with two cocks mounts. Or better still, I am the woman returning from shopping and boarding the bus with two roosters. Would the driver and passengers think, perhaps, that the roosters are my service or therapy animals rather than dinner?

Anyway, the roosters start crowing, and I look around for reactions. No one seems bothered. A lady in a purple suit in the row before us is applying makeup, her black high heels tapping the floor. She's carrying a trendy but fake Gucci handbag; what's supposed to be a gold chain looks rusted, and one G is nearly falling off. Two men on my right are on their smart phones. The one closest to me is looking at nudes, typing feverishly in the chat window, a broad grin on his face. The second guy is admiring a picture of two young boys in red jerseys posing with a soccer ball. Are they his boys or someone else's? Maybe he's their coach. His muscular and broad-chested body is bursting through the tight and sleeveless white jersey he's wearing. His head almost touches the taxi's roof. He could easily be six foot nine.

The woman with the roosters begins to doze, leaning into me occasionally. The taxi conductor shouts above Bebe Cool's music playing on the radio that we should start paying. I don't know the exact fare, so I give him a 2000-shilling note. He returns 700 shillings. While I'm putting the money in my bag, I see Murakami's *After the Quake*. I become aware of something shaking, only to see the nudes guy with a hand on his crotch. The expression on his face makes me pull out the book and start reading.

Lucky

I'm breastfeeding a chubby and giggly baby whose
name I do not recall. I can barely support her weight
on my chest. Sweat pools in my hands and elbows.

While I was away on a fellowship in Germany,
the baby had two mothers. I did not remember her.

I travelled to London and Spain. When I returned,
the nursing mother brought her home and said
she'd received the baby from another mother.

I resumed breastfeeding and was afraid she'd bite my
nipples with her sharp, erupting teeth. Even reject me.

She rubbed her mouth on my breasts, her gentle
breath caressing them before suckling. It felt
strange at first, but later, I began to like it.

She accepted my milk and love as though she had
no memory of being nursed by someone else.

As she fed contentedly, I looked at her flushed
face and envied her. Only two years,
and blessed with three mothers. Lucky girl!

Old Bartimaeus, I Feel You

In my version, when his
eyes opened and he saw
for the first time the hands
that had guided his movements,
he cried in astonishment,
I see! Dear Lord, I see!

Like me not knowing
who I was until the day
I touched myself
in the family photograph,
and screamed with the joy
of recognition all over my face.

The spark of vision
too marvelous, belief
comingling with disbelief
like a pupa finding light,
discarding its filmy
coat for the first time.

One Plus One Equals Three

There's a sweet daffodil girl in my home.
As soon as I enter, she bounces off the orange
sofa and follows me around the house.

Eyes fill with soft light as she smiles
at me, a smile so delicate and firm
like a moonbeam.

I think she's mine. Perhaps not,
but for now, I choose
to believe I am her mother.

One night she transforms
into three toddlers lying in their cribs,
identical like triplets.

They are a dazzling shade of bronze
that reminds me of David Černý's infants
caught in the sun's glint, but not barcoded

or marked in any peculiar way.
They are very pretty and adorably quiet,
one might think they are not breathing.

Devotion

It starts with a green shirt,
but before that is another beginning—

shall we say at a tea house or the lunch hour—
squash and asparagus, eggs and grits. Sitting

on the floor, legs outstretched, toes purposely
refuse to touch and spark woolen socks. It's winter, a

fire would be kind in the delicate conversation,
trading stories of urban and rural childhoods—

work in the town center, life on the farm, lifting
the weight of the moment like the hand that swiped

right, now pouring the rooibos into two blue cups,
the blue of the sea that resembles the eyes smiling.

How time speeds by in a moment of devotion
and the green shirt, coveted one Thursday evening,

hangs between hope and desire, gift and release,
a comma separating what could be one sentence—

that frightening word—sentenced to what might
become a bond of regret, a beautiful union.

There's mention of Pablo Neruda, as if he'd know
what to do with green, but the cost of the shirt bears

the burden of priceless. There would be more
lunches and dinners, requests and discussions

while the fate of the shirt, olive green, who gets
to keep it—casts a new beginning or dissolution.

The Goat, the City, the Embassy

It terrifies me to drive in Kampala City after being away for many years. Few traffic lights work, and when they don't, it's chaos. We share the potholed roads with goats, chickens, boda-bodas, pedestrians, buses, and public taxis springing from any direction. The most aggressive charge forth. I'm amazed accidents aren't frequent. Once in a while, you'll hear of a bus that crashed going upcountry, but rarely in the city. To boost my confidence, my sister says I must be pushy if I'm to move from point A to B. Otherwise, I'll be stuck in the same spot and irritate those behind me or trying to get ahead.

When it's time for my visa appointment at the American Embassy, I ask my sister to give me a ride. On our way we get trapped in a jam—a thicket of motorbikes and taxis honking, engines turning on and off, spewing black smoke. This is the work of Japan, selling used, decrepit cars to dreamers who'd never have thought of themselves in a position to own cars. I want to say something about the environment, the pollution, but to my left, I see a woman on a boda-boda hugging a black goat with a sack of potatoes tied behind her. I lower the window, and, without looking away, fish for my phone in the bowels of my large handbag. The cars start to move, the engines' roar scares the goat. It leaps out of the woman's embrace and lands on our hood. This is why I love this city! I clap ecstatically. Quickly pour the contents of my bag onto my lap and grab the phone to take a picture, but by then, the goat, the woman, and the vehicles ahead of this wild ecosystem have moved on. Behind us, folks are honking thunderously.

They Birthed Nations, Word Says

The women who could not bear children
            at first:

Sarai, Rachel, Rebekah, Hannah,
Samson's mother—name not given
Elisabeth—John the Baptist's mother
and Michal—the one that got away.

Their persistent asking
amidst improvisations
was the knowing
that they were capable,
deserving and worthy.
Such confidence!

Had they believed they were barren,
              truly,

they would not have   eventually
conceived.

Day and night they travailed
driven by the intensity of need,
the wretchedness of longing,
their hearts' desires to give life to—

      I hate to compare
      with my own hunger—
      a yearning that never goes
      away—to hold into my arms
      what I've made in love,

                    nurtured with love,
                    for months, years...

Like poetry, children
are not products but
life's fruit manifesting
in form, toil, and prayer.
In joy and quest,
the becoming—

a miracle that surprises
and sustains.

And so our heroines, their
eyes once blue and brown
turned red looking at what
could not be theirs—silently
cursing all the rug rats born
easily year on to year.

They even envied goats
all the fecund lot.

Naturally, bitterness crept
in while still refusing the evidence
of what was seen as—
                childless.

Not barren, their solid trust.
                Such faith!

The Lord in his air-conditioned,
meat-provided temple finally heard
their never-ending cassette cries.

Perhaps he got tired or bored.
He rose from his high seat and spoke:
You shall have what you ask for.

He remembered each
and opened their wombs   except Michal

He remembered each of them
    in their old age.

Let's stay with Sarai—
she couldn't haul her stricken bones
without her joints crackling—
confirmed crepitus.   Sagging breasts,
holed teeth.   Calcium gone.
So, she laughed!
               Let's be honest—
               who wouldn't?

She could not recall when
she'd last made love with Abraham—
that rascal of a husband who once betrayed
her to a pagan king? Lust counts. Still—

How was this child to be born?

The Lord of incongruity heard her laugh
and he sighed   for a second time.
Rose from his throne and paced a bit.
He'd have to find new messengers,
speak to that son-of-a- Abraham,
convince him to light a candle,
get some incense.
Myrrh— Abraham suggested.

Heck no.   That's for funerals.
Nobody dies. Find something
in remembrance of romance—
desert herb—rosemary
or sweet marjoram.

Suffice it to say that Abraham obeyed,
and shaved. In the absence of bottled
after-shave, he used cloves. Sarai glanced
at him and remembered their youth,
how she had loved and forgiven him.
He was wrinkly now   but he smelled nice!
Earthy and sweet. For a moment
he even looked like   beautiful.
She summoned whatever strength
left in her bones and made a special dinner—
lamb spiced with mint was his favorite,
crushed pistachios in the sauce. A basket
of barley bread. They'd eat together
in silence—that was it. The air
of resignation loomed.
That was it—no heirs.   End of a life.
They would have dinner

They were quiet for a while until
something stirred   in both.
Sarai's hand stretched across the table
Abraham reached out and held it,
smoothed the calluses, then kissed them.
She smiled and felt a fire, a bout of arthritis
and was about to withdraw the tingly hand
when Abraham raised it toward his lips,
again. He thanked her for the delicious meal.

Before she could say, We are old together,
Abraham whispered, Lie next to me.
And she did.

    A breeze from the east ruffled
their tent flaps and the two snuggled up.

    All those years of waiting,
all she'd ever wanted was to swaddle
a newborn. Hold it tightly in her arms.
Was that too much to ask?
Here she was, holding her elderly husband
instead. And then,   then
a quickening in her loins   in his loins
I-mpo-ssible, they almost said at once,   but
understood what was happening—
a mercy, at last.

And God was happy and demanded more meat
until Isaac was born.

A Very Short Story

Once upon a time, there was a child
who gave birth to a man and a woman.
The three lived together in a suburb
not unlike the suburbs we have today.

Life is freedom, the child would say.
Life is joy.

Then the child disappeared.

The man and the woman the child had
produced started looking for the child.
They knocked from door to door,
describing and asking everyone if any
had seen the child, but nobody had.

In their ceaseless search for the child,
the man and the woman gradually
forgot what the child had said about
the purpose of life.

Now, gray-haired, you can see them every
so often walking the suburbs, hoping
to catch a glimpse of the child, but also not
sure if they ever had a child to begin with.

The Shape of Light

The child survivor is having nightmares.
There's a demon coming down to take her.

She draws black figures against white ones to keep
the demon at bay. I do not know where she learnt this.

I look at her three black figures parallel to the three
white ones. She uses a *magnetic* pencil that sticks

wherever she puts it, and it moves at the slightest
touch in the direction she wants it to go.

Magic courses through her fingers to the pencil.
When she cries, I run to hold her in my arms.

I wrestle the pencil from her hand and set it down.
I want her to rest. I whisper in her ear that she's safe.

That she'll be safe, but she sees the future and it's dark.
Our polarized nation is at war within and without.

I carry her to my big brother's tent where we both
attend to her. When the demon returns, I pray.

The child draws with her fingers. I don't know what
my brother does, but he appears to be doing something.

When we put the child in bed, the demon leaves
as the last log in the fire crackles and spits.

Tasseography

The face of God swirls to the surface of Earl Grey.
Drink, it says, and then spins back to the bottom.

Undisturbed sediment. How like God, and, delicious,
flavored with the fragrant oil of bergamot. Unusual

too, to be addressed before the cup is drained,
the tongue licking sugar from the beggar's bowl.

On the rim, sorrow strings a rosary in the saints' temple
where the sacred and profane kneel to greet the Pope.

Once foretold, what's the querent to do but clasp
with devotion the inverse face of God in the left hand.

The Baby in the Priest's Room

In a small crib in the priest's home
is a baby, who looks like Anne's baby
girl, peaceful and sleeping while I'm
in the kitchen cleaning for hours.

When she stirs, I pick her up and hold
her until she falls asleep again. I put
her back into her cot in a room adjacent
the kitchen. Seven priests reside here,

and I wonder how a baby happens
to live with them. I'd like to finish
up and go to my family, but each time
I try to leave, there's something else

to tackle—cobwebs to wipe off
the walls, vacuum every corner, dust
the furniture... When at last I'm done
and putting the darling to sleep one more

time, she's grown so heavy I can't lift her.
I sort of drag her to a larger bed across
the room, and I'm thankful she keeps
smiling. Another baby could have cried.

Seven of Dragons

The water dragon is friendly.
She will trick you to test
the limits of your fantasy. You
summon her, and out of puffy
clouds every choice you could
ever dream of flows to you.
Jewels, castles, flowers,
and strong medicine to transmute
the darkness float in your eyes.
The partner you seek is in the air.
Come down, you sigh. Please,
come down. Shadows
in the pockets of your black
coat plead. But where shall you
keep the bounty and steer
clear of extremes?

In the Animal Kingdom, Mothers Feed First

Imagine giving birth to a child
you don't remember conceiving.

You're in an unfinished building
that has no windows or doors. All bricks,

big and sturdy with tall grass growing
around it. Once completed, it will be

a gorgeous house. You love the baby
but wonder how to break the news

to your family. They're not aware you
were pregnant. You've even startled your

boyfriend who now seems to be—
your husband? Anyway, the baby looks

healthy and beautiful. You're well too.
Just a little tired. Your husband expects

you to start cooking potatoes so that when
his brother visits, there will be food. You're

confounded he's making demands, as if he's
forgotten you've just given birth! Then he says

he's getting hungry as well. You let it slide
and go upstairs to take a nap, which turns out

to be deep and invigorating. Meanwhile, your
husband has also fallen asleep and when he

awakes, he suggests going to Red Lobster. You
grab your purse, kiss the baby, and head out to eat.

Overload

I'm driving a big and long truck that does not have good brakes, but I'm not afraid. I've just left my parents' house, and when I come close to a collision, a quick swerve saves life. Instead of stepping on the accelerator or brakes with one foot, I use both feet energetically in a clockwise movement as if I'm pedaling a bicycle. Soon, I'm going down a hill and pedestrians are crossing the road. I would like to honk, and that's when I realize the horn is close to my seat. It's cumbersome taking my hands off the steering wheel to squeeze the horn, but I have no choice. Whoever designed this truck lacked a fundamental comprehension of ergonomics.

It looks like market day on the road—folks carrying produce and shouting their merchandise—tropical fruits, vegetables, herbs, and spices. Some vendors are chatting and laughing without a care while walking or biking. Potters display their pots, dishes, jugs, and mugs on the roadside. Animals make their hungers and fears known—bleating sheep, grunting pigs, cackling chickens—and children crying. Cobblers announce tanned boots, sandals made of sisal, as well as their incredible skill mending shoes. As I approach a small church nearby, I wish to enter and sit in silence but a rooster crows, followed by bells ringing. Behind me, one biker is in danger of ramming into me. I put my head outside the window and ask him to keep his distance. He grins, speeds up to my side and starts a conversation—How long have I been driving the truck? Is it any good? Where am I going? Why am I not driving fast? This is bizarre! but for some reason, I do not ignore him. We talk and the tumultuous multitude no longer bothers me.

Abundance

While standing on the balcony
with my hands on the rails at seven
minutes past seven, I look up and count
three supermoons—grayish black—
followed by a fourth that's crescent
in a starry night like van Gogh's.
When the sun pops out, it's the size
of honeydew I've just harvested,
and waltzes round the moons.

Crowds of people arrive from town
to talk about hunting, but I'm
transfixed by the night's phenomenon.
I have no name for it. There's meat
in my fridge, and nearby, a grocery
store I trust. I keep nudging folks
to look at the moons now dancing
in alignment with the sun.

A boyfriend I don't remember
dating emerges to stand with me.
We watch the heavens shoulder
to shoulder, a harmonious wave
surrounding us like the infinite band
of orange light circling the moons.
Every few seconds, the celestial
bodies exchange positions.

October

October home lying on the equator,
we had plenty of rain and sunshine.
I don't remember
whether days were shorter or longer,
nights always ended fast.

Mornings broke with Dad
holding keys to the storehouse.
What shall we plant this season?
We were always selecting seeds,
planting, harvesting. Grazing livestock.

Today, I'm at the farmers market
in New York State. I see pumpkins, pies,
peas, potatoes, cabbages and cauliflower
my father loved to weigh in his hands.
How much does this cost?

I look into the Caucasian faces
but see my father. Always jolly,
proud of his crop.
Wiping at my eyes,
I go to the farmer with the largest stall.

That would be ours—
I'd be the girl under the table
picking more from the sacks,
arranging and replenishing
what I'm here to take home.

DEATH

The Diminishing Years

My father's face lingers and swallows
My childhood in a precious smile.
Thoughtful kindnesses, the memories
of diminishing years—gray and gold.
A ride on his bicycle. Permission
to put on his boots although they're
too big for me to walk in.

My father's voice whispers, This is how
you roast squash: You wrap it in tin foil
and bury it beneath hot ash. Go about your
business and when you're done, retrieve
the squash from the warm embers.
And this is how to iron a man's pants.
He puts hot charcoal in the flat iron,
presses, folds, and unfolds.
I'm only seven but I watch for hours
tasks I am sure to mess up as I grow.
The gray and gold, gold and gray merge
until all there is, is the grave.

My father's face swallows my present
More alive in death I remember him,
in life I do not forget him. He grows
on me daily, perforates my skin with his
presence so I can speak and answer that
I am present too—return to the love
that never left heals the overstretched self—
The space between is nothing, no-space,
a gap so artificial and yet real.

To have imagined I'd lost you
is now inconceivable.

Integration

It's taken me years to realize that the gray
trees in Pisgah Forest are ghosts.

Unlike people, dead trees do not give
up their spirits and collapse to the ground.

They remain standing for years, growing
grayer, skinnier, but maintaining position,
disguised tall among the living.

In a dream later, a haloed stranger with horse
hoofs says humans become ghosts long
before they die—we walk around with death
in our armpits, and when we fall sick, we're
steps closer, but it can take time for our ghosts
to gain full possession of what we assume
to be our spirits. Then the gleaming stranger
explodes into animal poo in front of me.

Startled into wakefulness, I do not rise
straight away but lie like an alligator,
wondering what else will stop me
from looking at another person as just human.

Things Have Been Disappearing

Things have been disappearing from my house. My husband was the last to go. He was wearing a green jersey and white tennis shoes. I don't remember him playing tennis. I think the last time I saw him was a Tuesday, maybe Wednesday. I'm not sure. I came home from teaching and found him gone. I made bean soup, put rice in the cooker, and waited. I cut some tomatoes. We liked them on the side. After the rice pot beeped, it stayed on warm, the soup on low. At 8:00 p.m., long past our dinnertime, I was hungry and served myself. The next day was the same: coming home, not finding my husband, making dinner, waiting, then eating. Washing the dishes, going to bed. On the third or fourth day, it occurred to me that he was gone. I put together a list of missing items: staplers, kitchen scissors, a box of steel-cut Irish oatmeal, a pack of rubber bands, a spice bottle of cinnamon, our purple bed sheets, my bathroom sandals, an orange armchair, a television, and the man.

My Father Is a Rainbow

I am conscious
    of falling into a dream
        I do not want
            but my attempt
                to not dream fails.
Darkness hovers over me,
and a hole opens in the center above my forehead.
My spirit begins to seep out, the color of liquid gold.
Then gray smoke. My body gets heavier
as I become lighter. After I've completely
left my body and merged with floating
consciousness, larger than life, I feel fine.

A woman whose intentions aren't clear
stands before me. Her features are hazy.
A voice says I'll need help to get rid
of her, and that help is available. All I
have to do is call the name of my
helper—a guardian spirit.

No name or angels spring to mind.
Close to despairing, I suddenly remember
my father James, and summon him three
times. He appears in a rainbow. Approaches
the woman, who begins to disintegrate
and dissolve into my dad. It's really cool
to watch. The rainbow expands.
I stretch my hands to touch my father
and ask a few questions, but he flies
away. It's clear without explanation

that he does not want to engage
in conversation or for us to touch.

In the morning, I awake with a throbbing
headache in the spot where the hole was. I
push my fingers into the aperture as if expecting
to grasp my brains or something, but all
is intact. At that moment my phone rings.
I have half the mind to disregard the call.
But then, I glance at the screen,
and see the name James.

The Nature of Opposition

Jupiter locates my comfort in the house
of endings—the stock market crashes,
the car dies, and the man barks.
Blooming trees shed their flowers.

We're like trapped ghosts housed
in houses, even when we go outside
into the woods or seas, our spirits
are still inside bodies within bodies.

At some point, Jupiter will enter Gemini
and influence my communication.
Earth will spin between Sun and Mars,
but it's my heart's trepidation I'll hear.

Mars is red. Very red. Rising at sunset,
it shines brilliantly all night and could be
mistaken for the sun if night were day. I
wonder if that's how it gets its name—

the god of war—desert cold and dusty,
rich in iron spoils, and visible at times.
Earth's motion casts Mars opposite the Sun
where astronomers see it clearly and declare

Mars in opposition to the Sun. Dramatic.
Rocky, without the butterscotch sweetness.
What about us—the people? Tiny insects
reeling. Yet still, important in all that.

I've Kept You Alive

Dad, you thrive in my dreams.
You fly on a magic carpet of colors. I wish
to join you, but you wave me away.

First, I see you falling from the sky. Looking
like a ship, large, mechanical, terrifying.
When you land at my feet, you transform
into an organism, a salamander. Even so,
you look more threatening than the ship.

As if you're hearing my thoughts, you decide
to become a lungfish with a large head. I
stroke your head, your eyes so beautiful.
You've evolved in your choice of breathing
organs and sound, equipped with extra lungs.
How perfect! No more fluid build-up,
oxygen therapy, or the pills you hated.

We laugh about how we both love eating fish.
We walk to my house which is big and made
of glass like a greenhouse. You do not use
the door, but squeeze in-between the wall
and floor, then crawl into the living
room. There's no telling your limits.

I step outside to call an aquatic company
that owns a swimming pool and specializes
in creatures like you. I want to buy you a tank.
I fidget with my phone and desperately press
numbers, which get erased the moment
they reach three. How to dial a full ten?

Eventually, I return to the room and find you've died in a blue bucket after chopping yourself to pieces. My sister appears and wants to cook you. I tell her you're not a fish! A slice of salmon materializes and my sister says, Some fish are red, others whitish-brown—which is the color you are now. Like tilapia, she adds. I don't see her point, although, I feel less troubled.

Transit 11 11

She appears like a blot of blood waltzing across
the Sun's face, daring and steady the movement she
makes—the movement that marks Mercury's transit
between Earth and the Sun. We would go blind to look
without protecting our eyes. Fear of trespassing
cascades down my spine and spills into the ground
decorated with yellow and red remembrances
of veterans. Around the tree trunks, their blood
and service. Today we remember our loved ones who
dared to look the enemy in the eye, who knew
protection by putting their lives on the line, gone like
mercury in the hot sands of history. Thirteen years
from now, this tiny body in the sky will step
on the giant blood orange again, unafraid. The fire
she crosses will not consume her. Flesh of her flesh
unburned. We are told she shrinks but it's not her
time to die in the flames. She will return to remind us
that she'll outlive us. I look into the sky and pray
to remember the significance of this moment, this
event mixing with death that we tell ourselves is
honorable, permitting us to plant poppies and crosses
in fields of bones and cold concrete commemorated
in barbed wire hearts. Mounted telescopes in the quad
call us to witness   to observe with   reverence.
Even in our volatile circuits and tilts we do not
abandon the post. Thirteen years from now—how
many will be dead? And who will be at the observatory
standing where we are—watching this wonder
repeating once more, this small, rocky planet covered
with craters in her passing hours of magnificence?

Leonard Cohen Saves the Maiden

An old woman with two front teeth missing
is swishing her hands, making scooping
gestures to harvest my shadow.

I keep moving, avoiding her,
but she knows how to find me
in my parents' yard. If she

captures my shade,
she'll do anything. Even kill me.
I pray the sun to go down, but
who knows what tricks she has.

I summon one of my exes—the one I sent
on his way with best wishes—appears
and distracts the old woman with a Leonard
Cohen song about the darkness, my escape.

Dad Is Happy Drinking Beer in Heaven with Uncle Malcolm

My father and Uncle Malcolm are sitting on a rustic bench drinking beer on St. Patrick's Day. They look youthful, handsome, spirited. Even dimpled! Holy gods, they're the age unknown to me except in photographs.

    Their laughter pulls me out of the adjoining room, but a geyser of steam spurts from the walls, and heat
       intercepts me from crossing the misted realm.

               I stand in the doorway and chat.
In my left hand, I notice I, too, have a beer. I take a sip but keep the hand hidden. I'm a teenager.
Would they mind?   Later, when I wave goodbye, they see the bottle but make no fuss.

  Stepping outside, the malachite mountains proclaim, Alive is great, but dead is mineral
     where I dare not linger.

The Movement of Bodies

My body was buried without a heart—having donated it along with the left kidney and brain to the state. But I feel whole. I'm kept busy with new arrivals. My job is to welcome them, tell them to feel at home. Forget what they say about St. Peter minding the door. He's never here. I do not know who I am exactly. I wear a purple gown with buttons in front. When it gets hot, I unbutton. In a corner lies a bundle of clothes I was buried in: A green scarf, a beige dress, and white shoes. I remember owning the dress and scarf, but not the shoes. Since I stay on my feet a lot, I wear Vibram Five Fingers. They're comfortable. There's plenty of dust and no mirrors. I would like to tell you about the others—what they do and say—but once I check them in, I don't hear a thing besides the swinging door. I stand in the doorway and say, Welcome! Hand the new arrivals a change of clothes which are mysteriously placed in my arms. Then step aside and let them enter the great hall. As they move, fog appears suddenly and swallows them. Hot or cold, fog is omnipresent.

Chthonic

In this other life, Mam is married to my dad.
        In this other life, Mam has mental illness,
                but Dad still dies first.

This evening, she wears a beautiful indigo dress
        embroidered with white lace across her chest.
                She's slender and eats very little.

When urged to eat more, she says she's married,
        meaning, if she gains weight, her husband
                won't find her attractive.

She sips wine with a teaspoon and pushes away
        the plate of food. Then she goes to her room
                and puts on a lot of clothes.

She looks like a tent. I ask our house-help to assist
        me in taking them off. We have to sedate her
                to do so. Then we bathe her.

We don't have a bathroom but make do with the small
        shelter in our backyard. First, we heat water
                and pour it on a basin in the shelter.

While scrubbing her, we see a young, green crocodile
        in the garden raising its head, watching us.
                I'm afraid it might latch onto us.

My helper says not to worry, this type is harmless.
        I'm not convinced. When we're done, we
                rush Mam to her room.

Dad is out and when he returns, I run to Mam
>   to tell her Dad is home. He goes straight to his
>   own bed and locks the door.

I keep knocking, asking him to spend time with Mam.
>   Eventually he opens the door and walks away.
>   We do not find out where he lives.

Next thing we hear—he's dead in the backwaters
>   of the alligator. Mam has the last laugh,
>   ends up outliving everyone.

The Sink

Things easily corrode
with a little neglect.
Consider the sink—
a few days without
rubbing or scrubbing,
its luster begins to fade.

Weeks later, the color
you once knew is
replaced by a sickly, no,
deathly shade. The shine
gone like a body drained
of blood. Anemic sink.

If you ignore it,
the sink will continue
to rust away—a crust
of dust and dirt coats
the surface, death hangs
in the air like a comma,

leaving a slim chance
for intervention. You
can still rescue the sink.
Cleaning restores its life.
Perpetual neglect
brings the comma down.

Austerity

In hell, people drink
black coffee
day and night.

There are no chairs.

Souls lean against shiny
granite counter tops
holding thin paper cups
instantly refilled.

They talk and mingle,
their voices hoarse—
stuffing the room
with coffee-stained breath.

A joker reads their
cups and announces
they're in hell.
No one believes him.

Vendors arrive selling
used clothing. Excitement
builds as people try them
on, but buy nothing.

They have no money.
This happens every Friday.
It's the only way
they get to see color.

A Place of Burning

He grew tired of painting her and decided to kill her. A project dangling, he'd once introduced her to his fellow artist. She thought he'd meant what he was painting. He would kill her with his brush, colors, and sand. As was the routine, she undressed and sprawled on the couch. He'd begin from anywhere—that's how inspiration worked, he explained. For three years she lay naked on the orange couch and watched him applying brown hairs to her pubic region, cinnamon on the lips, then skip to her buttocks or legs.

Today he changed her lips to ruby, which wasn't the color of her lips, and the crimson kept running down, down, until it was her blood. He remade the hair fiery red too, yet she was a brunette. Her eyes widened in fear. He told her to look away while he worked on her neck, slightly turned. With sharp strokes he transformed her into death's grotesque mask consumed in a sheet of flames. Burning. He'd known death to be intense, but he hadn't expected it to be red. He had a wicked grin when he said she was finished.

Glancing at the image, she shrieked and rushed out of his house without her clothes. She kept running, screaming, and folks pursued her. When finally they caught up with her, someone threw her a scarf, another a shawl, another a jacket, until she was a bundle of clothes. The kind folks led her home, a lovely cottage she had purchased with hard-earned cash from modeling. She stumbled on the cobblestones that covered the path to her door, and a soft hand steadied her. She spent the rest of her days in solitude, a deranged look replaced her once lively hazel eyes.

The artist's painting sold for six figures and then some. When the top collectors couldn't afford to bid anymore, museum after museum purchased it. I saw it in the Musée du Louvre, but by then, the artist, not knowing how to handle the success, had exchanged his miserably famous life for the fires of Hades.

Winters

Christmas mood? My father asks on the telephone.
It's getting darker and darker. Is it even four yet?
The day looks like it has forgotten its light makeup.
Never seen a day the color of soot. A time for bears
to hibernate. A few weeks ago we turned our clocks
back, which makes no sense for him on the equator.

If only I could wear my father's trench coat
and walk in his boots, bending, falling, but happy
to be warm. I wouldn't feel this heaviness
alone, and he'd have something wise to say.
He'd understand the gloom, an ominous cold
that may not be that strange to him.

At dusk, I look up, then left, right, and the sky
is a map of blackness without boundaries.
The sliver of the moon smiling faces away from me.
I envy the sky its spaciousness, breathing with ease,
merging with night, while I struggle through the day.
Locals say, This is only the beginning in Syracuse.

Does It Get Better?

In my desperation to understand what could not be understood by anyone else, I googled *Ten best ways to die*. You won't believe how many pages popped up. Death by hanging, swallowing pills, drowning... among the worst methods. Don't try it. Tell me instead what it's like to hang onto this life and drink every bit of juice in it. The desire to outlive the baobabs and redwoods should the gods be that merciful. When you get right down to it, can be a good life. Requiring little to love— a pat on the back, a baby's grin while pushing its fat finger between your lips, the smell of good coffee! Some days, of course, we plunge into the dark sea. Tell me how to conjure up a field of sunflowers. Aren't they gorgeous in the meadows? To lie still. Listen and repeat. The imagination making the world. Ringing like a doorbell—lusty and persistent. Asking again and again, to visualize putting the feet on the ground, feeling the steady pulse of this body coming to life.

Blazing Wild

    Eyes of a dog on fire

Coming down the burning mountain

Ignores the creek nearby

    Clears the path ash-white.

The gaze—

    Intent and dying

        Life and fury fused,

        Wispy smoke—the air

    Singed wood   grass   and fur

Beyond the scope

Of racketing helicopters

Coughing   water.

Father

After Robert Hayden's "Those Winter Sundays"

Forgive us—
Father

The gourds you brought home
for our protection embarrassed us.

Our Catholic mother suggested
we throw them into the river.

You watched quietly and did not interfere
as we carried away your treasures.

Betrayed our ancestry. How could you
stand us in the business that was not ours?

What did we know, Father, what did we know
of your silent wisdom and the pain we caused you?

Komorebi

In winter, a sharp light
breathes through naked trees, sky, and snow.
Oh, the difference it makes! My melancholy lifts.
Smiles appear on cracked lips of strangers in the park.
Beneath crunching footsteps, earth vibrates.
But make no mistake—it's not yet time
to take off layers. The bluest sky is a poison, a refrain.
Not less or more, but what's required
to bridge over the figure standing next to me.

To bridge over the figure standing next to me—
not less or more, but what's required
to take off layers. The bluest sky is a poison, a refrain.
But make no mistake—it's not yet time.
Beneath crunching footsteps, earth vibrates.
Smiles appear on cracked lips of strangers in the park.
Oh, the difference it makes! My melancholy lifts
dancing through naked trees, sky, and snow
in winter's sharp light

Hands in Clay

My father grows lovelier each day
I do not see him, each year
I cannot see him. My mind activates
and remakes him in vivid and memorable
palettes capable of fitting new lenses. All
the best parts stand out. The not-so-great
fall off like clods of clay. Grayish
remains to be cleansed by living
organisms, refined by cremating fire.

Like decomposition, the mind is
excellent at repurposing and paring
to bones and ash while extracting the essence,
singing golden. Searching for synonyms,
the thesaurus adamantly changes *cremation*
to *creation*, which makes sense of this
threshold, my heart wintered like the pale
bark of an aspen. When is hope in the inky
strokes of a misty sky holding back tears?

Air so raw and dark blots threatening rain,
witnessing the work I am molding in this
frozen circle saturated with longing.
Other than a drop or two, all is contained
like dish water in a plugged silver sink.
At night, the waxen moon is my father's head
poking through. Maybe mine. Blake was right—
everything is through—as in *veil*, if not *vale*.
But this fog, my God, I am not through.

REBIRTH

There's No Present but the Past and Future from Which We Create

The moon will take position in my tenth house this chilly evening. I'm supposed to understand what that means but I don't. Only aware of a sadness settling into my chest like a new camper, sucking my breath, zapping momentum.

I remember a dream I had the previous night—an aggressive black cow, skinny and gaunt, charging at my sister. Our parents are divorcing—a great shock. But why are we dividing the clothes? Who gets to keep the house with its antique feng shui furniture?

Suddenly, I find myself at Dulles International Airport and my last stop will be Syracuse, but I end up in a restroom. A lady with short hair appears and takes me to her quarters. Two small bottles of Fireball Cinnamon Whisky sit on her coffee table in the living room.

Why is it called a coffee table when it can hold other things? The lady tells me we are in Chicago and pours me a drink, but I run outside to find my way home. The lady transforms into my younger sister and follows me. I rush back inside and latch the door.

In the morning when I awake, I call home to speak with my parents and ask why they'd throw away 47 years. They laugh, taking me lightly as usual, which annoys me. I talk to my siblings and they, too, tell me to quit dreaming and get a life, as if.

House of Moab

What meaning
left behind
or curved inside
petrified dunes?

Speak, oh memory
trapped in rocks.

Ancient faces
in the canyons,
in the arches
of our ancestors
watching over us.

The sun,
silent witness
to what we see
or do not see—
The living-dead
etched in stone
in desert spaces.
So we name them
The Three Gossips,
the Dark Angel,
Head of a Sheep...

What is it that compels
us to dream and name
these seemingly breathing
shapes, if not to give
life, to find
meaning—
a door.

Loved

you are loved
body and soul
but cannot express
          your true nature,
          your appetites hidden
the hallelujah grows cold on your tongue
broken, lonely,
a radiant melancholy.

but you open up
in your poetry,
          feeling the hum of your body cells
          ticking, knocking against the ribcage,
the energy of your heartbeat
intention in your fingertips
dissecting emotions
looking specifically for joy.

you are loved considerably
your connection divine
attend
          to your mind like marble sails,
          the pillars of your heart shine
alive with light like
a bright alabaster jar.
no hair on your head
now but a spherical,
translucent glass
moving in light,
reaching out in
sensuous beauty,
luminous, numinous
immeasurable you.

The Tower Falls

No one knows who started the fire.
The crew came four hours late
for the question—to put out the flames
or let the tower tumble?

All the records burnt down but two
people escaped. Nobody got hurt.
The fire is always invisible at first.
Inevitable, some say, for destruction
and creation go hand in hand.

Loss to vent, but how to let go
of what we've built—symbols
of success, structures, and beliefs
of what we've become. How to recall
we're not concrete or the sand
between bricks and stones
for new shapes to be revealed—
purified and deposited at the banks
like rich ash from which to plant
new seeds. How do we get better
releasing the shatters of what no
longer nourishes, and looking
through the void of blackened
windows for light and spaciousness?

The shift is never sudden. Rather,
the force of what hits us—awareness

recognition of what is as opposed
to what appears to be—confusion,
anguish, and pain with an intensity
beyond the scale of one to ten.
What else counts?

Time. Tests everything. Sadly.
Mercifully. In the end, Freedom
illuminates the crown of Surrender.
On what ground can we stand
when fire purges, erases,
and cleans like water?

You Are Here—on a Map

The comforting presence of trees
        grounds me.
On one of the trails with a waterfall,
        I sit on an ancient rock
              and think fondly of you, father,
surrounded by what you loved—clean air,
the trickling sound of a gentle creek,
a flourishing forest.

After all, my journey is about finding you,
rather than leaving. Joining all the old things—
timelessness, rocks over a billion years old,
and venerable trees whose rings
will one day speak of our times'
ecological forces shaped
by Hurricane Helene.

You'd be eighty-four today. Now I
understand why my people
call the dead
our ancestors. Like the mountains,
the uplifting of the earth's tectonic plates,
we raise them up
each time we remember them.

Climbing a Giant Waffle-like Building and Meeting a Witch

is a great challenge. Instead of stairs or ladders, each of us must step into narrow spaces between bricks, and clamber up to the rooftop. Imagine a tall, kiln-like square waffle! It gets trickier where some rows have zero space in-between, but we're not discouraged easily.

When I'm close to the corner wall and left with a few blocks to reach the wide, flat top that offers a view of the sprawling village valley, I realize I'm out of spaces for my feet. Leaping upwards is out of the question. I think of going back down as I'm about to lose my grip. My fingers and palms are sweaty, but removing them from the wall to rub against my clothes would be suicidal.

One of my friends already at the top suggests I crawl toward the middle section like an ant and follow his steps. That's when I wish I had claws. After several awkward movements, I arrive. There's a kitchen gray with smoke, detached from the main house like in my childhood.

We sit around the fire chatting and preparing food. My eyes focus on a young woman shelling fresh beans and peas incredibly fast, dropping them into a large bowl. An old woman in rags appears and snatches the bowl, then flees. I chase after her and she laughs like a hyena in my face. Yawning gaps between her teeth. I threaten to harm her when I run out of persuasion.

I have a knife tucked in my underpants and waste no time pulling it out. She dares me to use it. It's getting dark as I stare at her twitching nose. She has power, we both know it. Could she be the reason we are here?

The Tools We Carry

This happens at Wash Park. Through the sextant's eye,
the sun is lime green and sits on top of the lake. Every
four seconds it moves while we are still on the bench.

Folks come and go. Geese poop, eat, and squirrels pick
nuts off the trees. We are here and there, in space
and time, measuring distance, speed, and altitudes.

The man with a red hat sitting next to me says,
It's not the sun that moves but earth rotating.
Since we're on earth, we don't see it circling the sun.

We hold the reversed image of the sun in motion
and that's the magic of science—what is and what
appears to be—a source and the apparent source.

I begin to wonder if one could fall asleep, and wake
up as someone else. A simulacrum orbiting without
breaking sequence, yet never forgetting what is or isn't.

There's the sun and sunlight. Light and the light
source all at once. I'm a friend of fractals refraining
from charting the course, bearing in mind refraction.

When we say the sun moves from east to west, where
are we (in motion) finding center and decentering?

The Fire People

We've turned our walks
into finding things
that catch fire easily, like us.
Our fascination with bush craft—
how to survive in a forest
without the conveniences
we have at home.

The first human to discover fire
rubbed two stones together.
Friction is a good thing.
We have fun starting fires,
scratching the Mora knife
against the small iron rod,
sending sparks into a nest
of dried grass and fibrous barks.

You put out the flame
with the sole of your hiking boot
so we can begin, again.
By the time we leave the forest,
we've discovered deer poo combusts
easily, human hair does not. I've
given a lock and you've won the bet.
By the time we leave, we've lost
count of the fires we've started.

Letting Go

The silver Volvo is
cleaned, personal
belongings removed—
a hawk feather, a coffee
mug, an ice scraper.
Soon, the tow will take
it away to the seed bank—
a donation. Save
memories of travel,
bed and board
in that car—
spontaneous trips to Moab,
the Rocky Mountains,
and now, a lost lover,
a detour in the bend.

The Colorado River
must be what it's like
to let go,
what lingers
and flows—the final
goodbye.

Freedom is
but Lord,
what we give up
for wings to flutter
and take off!

What's mine
will surely find
a way to return—
There's hope
Delusion
Prayer
Release—the car,
the man,
the times to cling
turned loose.

Between Wake and Sleep in the Heart of the City That Delights and Shatters

A short distance from where I stand is a humongous mall that's eaten up all the space. The small buildings around it look cramped and uneasy, as if they're struggling to breathe. I stare at this city that's running out of room, constantly changing—growing, declining, evolving, and dissolving. Would you believe among the many terrors that plagued my life in the past is Novinophobia—the fear of running out of wine? This city takes up space. Swallows everything—buzzing motorcade, ambulances, and a throng of pedestrians going in and out of the mall. And like love, it endures. I like being here reliving old and new memories. The past and present—a recurring future. Mixed company!

The city never closes. By nightfall, I'm surrounded by a silence that hums and makes me tender, feeling affection for ghosted loves in the nook of my elbows. Much as there's reason for fear, I need not worry about boundaries, limitations, or death—trappings of my imagination's worst scenarios.

The mind opens   severs   reopens.
I can see that now as I stand on this street that once housed my favorite cafe. I have no idea where it moved to. Perhaps just folded. In its former place is the ugliest fuel station. Diesel fumes and the red dust of this badly

patched city assault my nostrils as if to say, We are here doing all right. We mingle. We are not a fiction. We are true. We are expansive and not deserters. We do not run out. Why not rejoice in the choice to jump, to taste chances, to sit at the table and break bread for a little while before disappearing into the dawn? What shatters is also what delights and expands the heart. With the sound of the city in my head, I'll cross the road to the carpentry workshop, sit and hold hands. Estranged hands. Until the strangeness of what haunts vanishes.

The Boy Who Loved

Some day he imagined he'd be dead
and understand the nature of stars—
perhaps sit amongst them the way he sat
with cows around the fire. His days began
wet with dew and ended bright with stars.

Mornings were covered in dense fog—
he couldn't see the hills, and his hair
shimmered white with mist. He made
a fire and boiled water, which he used
to warm the cows' teats before milking
them. He drank the milk with his family,
then set off to graze in the open fields.

At night when it became unbearably
cold, he gathered logs and lit a big fire
for the cows. The cows would lie
by his side, frisking their tails
and chewing cud. What a comfort
to hear them breathing, belching,
smelling their smells—cud and dung.

What a delight to gaze into the sky—
contemplate the stars, wrapped in tingling
pleasure and awe. The stars watching
the night with him. Always shining.
Numerous. Held in careful suspension
so they'd not bump into his world.
A marvel, the order of the universe.
Could it be that he, too, was implicitly
known and loved, held like the stars,
like the cows, like the burning logs,
all in communion with the universe?

Piano Lessons

I

This happens in the sands of Dakar, Senegal.
My instructor Barry tells me to pay attention to the intervals. Before he leaves, he asks, Am I not afraid to be alone? I tell him there's always sound—ocean waves, the muezzin's call merging with kora music from the boutique stores, bleating sheep on the streets—resisting slaughter—and overloaded skinny donkeys mingling with honking cars as they cross the road by my window. But what's my sound? The reason he's here. He advises that I get an eye at the door to see through when someone buzzes. I must appear vulnerable to him. He is very vulnerable to me.

II

Majors and minors can be mixed. Anything can be played so long as you master the rules first. You can even play on the border of things and transition between the rules. Experiment with edge. I like that very much. It excites my body, my fingers, and opens my heart. Once you begin to feel the music, Barry says, you can play your own thing. It's about feeling, intervals, laws. At that moment my body tingles with new music and warm, courageous notes. I spread my hands over his, breaking laws that separate us or perhaps aligning until he, too, transposes down an octave to enjoy the shift from familiar to unfamiliar sounds we make together.

To Bury a Fire

We banked a fire that outlived our children. It boiled our water, cooked our food, and kept us warm. After dinner, before we slept, we collected black wattle logs, which were good at retaining flames in their heartwood. I learned to push a log beneath hot coal and ash, topped with cold ash to prevent the log from burning all the way. Other times I'd scoop red coals to one side, place a tight log in the hollow, then heap the embers back onto the log which would smolder through the night. By morning, a portion of the wood or cinders would be glowing. Add scraps of dried grass and sticks, watch the fire roar to life.

Pieces of wood retained heat for many moons. We thanked God for little things—the gift of breath to blow on a dying fire and see it rising, catching twigs. Stoking fires with the bellows of our mouths. Children were born, grew up, and married. More children from the marriages grew up and got their own children who got other children, and the fires burned steady and bright. We told the children who had become men and women how so and so's fires were older than them. They aspired to grow as old as the oldest fires.

We lived in the valleys and made supper around six o'clock when we came down the hills where we cultivated crops. We ground millet and sorghum on the grindstone for bread and porridge. We shelled peas, corn, and beans. When there was a rabbit or goat, Papa skinned it. Mother cleaned and cut up the meat, sweet potatoes, and squashes. My brothers split wood. We all took turns cooking and recounting the days' events around the fire. Our elders smoked pipes and told us stories that spread laughter across the hills and valleys, stirring admiration and sometimes envy. They thrived on echoes of joy that made us happy. But the most important thing growing up was to know how to rekindle a fire.

Growing Up

My tiny baby is swaddled in yellow clothes. The next
time I look, she's filled out, grown elastic
and wriggly when I try to contain her in my arms—
spilling out and smiling at me with her disarming
baby smile. She tells me her goal is to evolve
child-like as if she's
made of air and rubber.

                    She grunts like a piglet
                 when she's eating and points
            a finger at me to not get in her way.
      She can't talk properly yet,
but she's bent on mothering me. Nods when I'm
talking to adults like she's approving. Like she
understands. When she crosses her arms, she
instructs me to do the same. *The child is father
to the man,* she says, and squeals.

Won't it be fun to see me holding myself
like she does, and watching at the same time as
a separate entity stripped of all I thought I knew?

The Wisdom of Sea Cucumbers

When stressed or under attack, sea cucumbers expel their internal organs—viscera—an act known as evisceration. Days later, they regenerate the organs lost, which might include the gut, vessels, tentacles, anterior portion of the body wall, and strands of gonad. We talk of writing that's visceral—cutting to the marrow. Nowadays, I don't throw that word around unless my organs are truly involved.

Imagine possessing the ability to contract your body wall muscles acutely, causing abdominal cavities to tear and the anus to open as you release an organ while telling your aggressor: There's my kidney. I leave you my liver, and so on, as you walk away. Imagine how powerful your defense.

In other uses, to eviscerate is to deprive something of its essential content or force. To surgically disembowel. There's a Dutch band that goes by the name, *Eviscerated*. I suggest you do not listen to it. Besides surgeons and skilled torturers, ancient Egyptian embalmers eviscerated bodies of the dead—a crucial part in the rituals of mummification.

I ate sea cucumbers for the first time in Guangzhou, China, thinking they were sea vegetables. I enjoyed the mushroom-like texture in my mouth, rubbery, and filling. Later, on Skype with a friend, I told him about my dinner, and he laughed. Intrigued, I googled *sea cucumbers*. I almost threw up, but why did their lack of a brain bother me the most?

The Future

A friend of mine has this cool, electric,
silver shiny, rocket-like Audi she's
driving. She sits opposite me, facing
me as one would on a bus, not looking
straight ahead like a person at the wheel.
Much as I'm anxious about safety, the car
moves smoothly as it reads my friend's
gestures. She has great linear control
and a good sense of direction. I admire
her capability to navigate this large city
with four lanes on each side even when
she's not in the driver's seat. This must
be one of those autonomous vehicles I've
heard of, but not experienced before.
In front of us is a small screen live-streaming
the latest publications of poetry. I don't
recognize any of the poets, who address
auto sensibilities—'self' + mobile,
the self in motion and other combining
forms. The car autofocuses. Brief auto
analyses describe the science as *driven*,
moving, *nerve-racking*... all of it
automatically happening. The poets'
autographed copies are available!
The transmission ends with a quote:
To drive or be driven is the new question.
Dang! I've been told that the self is
responsible in all things, including

accidents, but which self since the car is
all auto? Driven by the need to find out, I
press the glowing red button and my friend
yells, What do you think you're doing?
First, we want control, and then we don't.

Beans

Beans came back. Always,
whenever she ventured far

from home. They spread
into her cold room with zest,

and kept multiplying. Some
burst through their pods

and climbed the bedpost.
When she touched them,

her hands warmed up. I love
you beans, she whispered,

and buried her face into their
robust stalks. The beans smiled

through their eyes. Each had
a tiny eye on its side. If she

pinched or pulled it, the bean
would split. But she wasn't

going to do that. Instead,
she embraced the beans again

and again, feeling their vitality
connecting with her roots.

Sanctum

Three male turkeys
have claimed
our holy space
in the woods—
the drum circle.
I approach cautiously,
each inhale purified
by the scent of pines
and fragrant blossoms
of black locust,
a hint of honey
on the nose.

The first time
I came here,
I sat on the big,
rugged rock.
At call and response,
tired hands and feet
felt the surge
and began
stomping until
the heart could
not separate
from the drumbeats.

At solstice, we speak
no other language

all night long.
Isn't it possible
we've found
at last, what the sages
meant when they said
we shall transcend
in the communion
of our souls—
as we linger
in unison?

These Moments

Sound—
the gentle hum of traffic
and my old fridge
thrumming its own chords—
Soothing and compelling me
to abandon duty for turtle
doodles that litter my table.

Hearing expands to receive
messages from my ancestors
several generations back,
and new locomotives
from the future—rumbling
steel with eyes of the tiger
glowing with perception.

I taste the purity of air
coming in from the mouths
of seals and salmons before
plastics entered the ocean.
All at once, I am a child
on the shore. I am the child
tending calves in the green
fields of my country, strong
winds rousing the trees
and the waves, attending
to me like an urgent lover—

Whoosh! Whoosh. Whoosh.

In these moments stretching
into infinity, I am an infant
yet full of years. Shedding
hair, teeth, and fully aware
that when my time arrives,
I'll take nothing. At cremation,
the body splinters into sparkling
fragments carried skywards,
iterative cells knowing which
way to go home—to a multitude.

18 Notes to Finish

After Derek Walcott's "Love After Love"

When I arrive home from a long walk,
I open the door and tell my presence, enter.
I fetch a Cabernet from the cabinet, and a tall,
Graceful glass. I step out of the kitchen,
Sway into the living room, sit with me.
Pour a glass, taste, and drink. A honeyed
Fragrance like fresh mulch rises to meet
me. Earthy notes, blackberry finish.

I run fingers across my hands and arms
Years of shea butter have softened the skin,
Even the elbows speak tenderness.
I sip the years that are yet to come,
and lovingly gaze into the person I have become.
Welcome home, I announce to myself, nodding.
Like the wine, full-bodied, mature, loneliness
Leaves no sourness on my palate but delectable calm.
Time swells and collapses on itself while I am here,
Keeping my own company, feeling enough.

ACKNOWLEDGMENTS

Acknowledgment to the following publications in which versions of these poems first appeared:

Annulet: "Seven of Dragons"

Braided Way Magazine: "You are Here—on a Map"

The Decolonial Passage: "I've Kept You Alive"

Diode Poetry Journal: "In the Animal Kingdom, Mothers Feed First" and "Cycles"

Hole in the Head Review: "Leonard Cohen Saves the Maiden" "Loved" "The Movement of Bodies" "The Tools We Carry" "The Wisdom of Sea Cucumbers" and "18 Notes to Finish"

Lolwe: "The Goat, the City, the Embassy" "To Bury a Fire" "Between Wake and Sleep in the Heart of the City That Delights and Shatters" and "Roosters, Taxi, and Murakami"

Moving Worlds, A Journal of Transcultural Writings: "October" and "The Sink"

Obsidian: "Father"

Orca: "The Future"

Poetry Quarterly: "The Diminishing Years" and "The Fire People"—reprinted on poets.org.

Sistories: "The Baby in the Priest's Room," "Abundance" and "Lucky"

Still: The Journal: "These Moments," "Sanctum," and "Old Bartimaeus, I Feel You"

The Poetry Review: "Things Have Been Disappearing"

The Progressive: "Transit 11 11"

Truck: "Overload"

Twenty-two Twenty-eight: "The Things You Encounter in Flight" "Tasseography" and "The Tower Falls."

"Piano Lessons" in *Capitals: Poetry Anthology*, ed. Abhay K. (Bloomsbury Publishing, 2017).

"Komorebi" in *Dead of Winter III Anthology*, ed. Kim Jacobs-Beck (Milk and Cake Press, 2024)

Mildred Kiconco Barya, a North Carolina-based writer and poet of East African descent, teaches and lectures globally. She is the author of four poetry books, including *The Animals of My Earth School* (Terrapin Books), which was listed a Brittle Paper Notable African Book of 2023 and received honorable mention in the 2024 Eric Hoffer Poetry Award. She is the recipient of the 2025 Jacobs/Jones African American Literary Prize for the best essay and the 2020 Linda Flowers Literary Award. Barya has served as the Gilbert-Chappell Distinguished Poet for the North Carolina Poetry Society and her work has been published in the *New England Review, The Cincinnati Review, Shenandoah, Tin House, The Forge,* and elsewhere. *Hands in Clay* is her fifth full-length poetry collection.

www.mildredbarya.com

www.ingramcontent.com/pod-product-compliance
Lightning Source LLC
Chambersburg PA
CBHW060536080526
44586CB00012B/753